A

B B B B

B B B B B

D D D D D D D D D D D D D D D D D D D D D D D

C C C

E

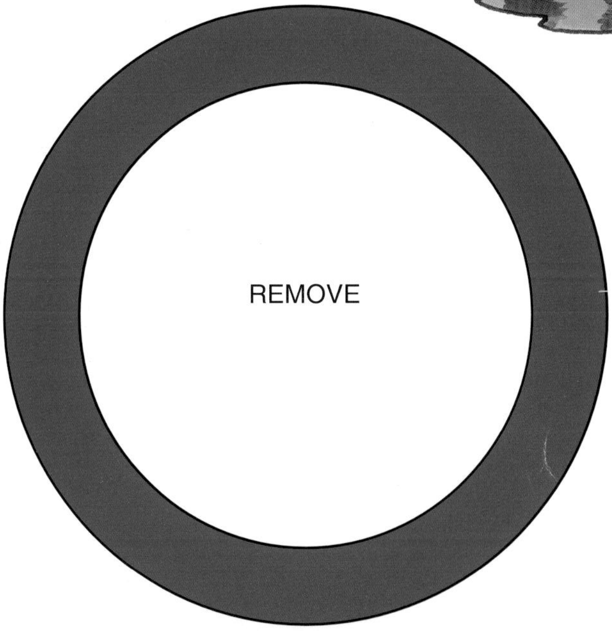

REMOVE

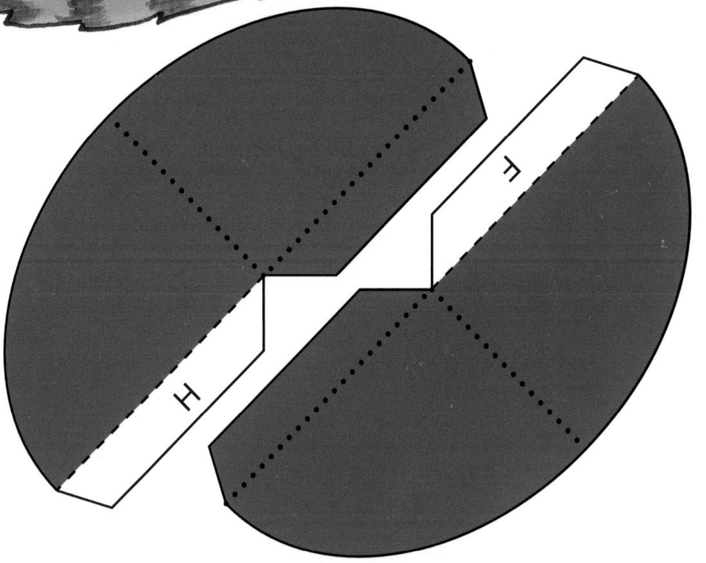

F

H

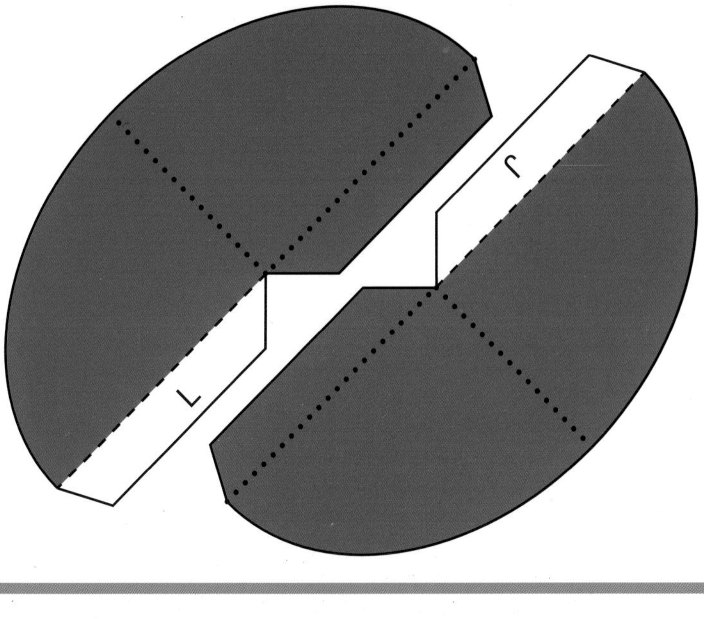

J

L

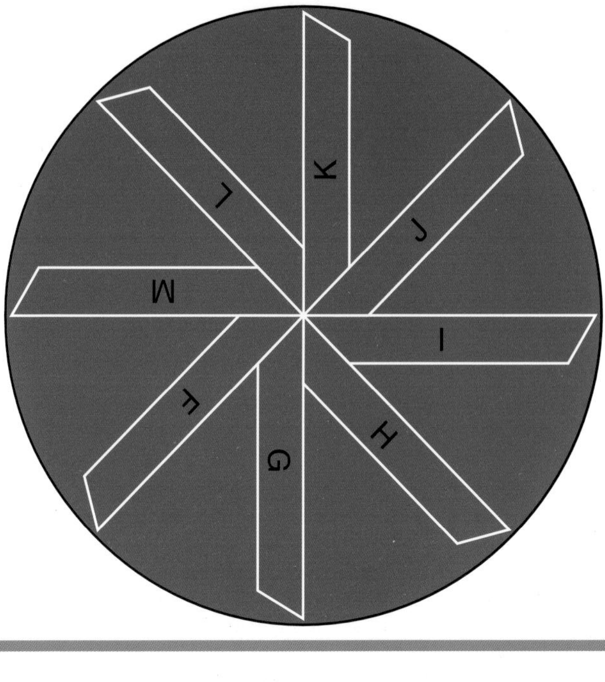

K

J

L

M

I

F

H

G

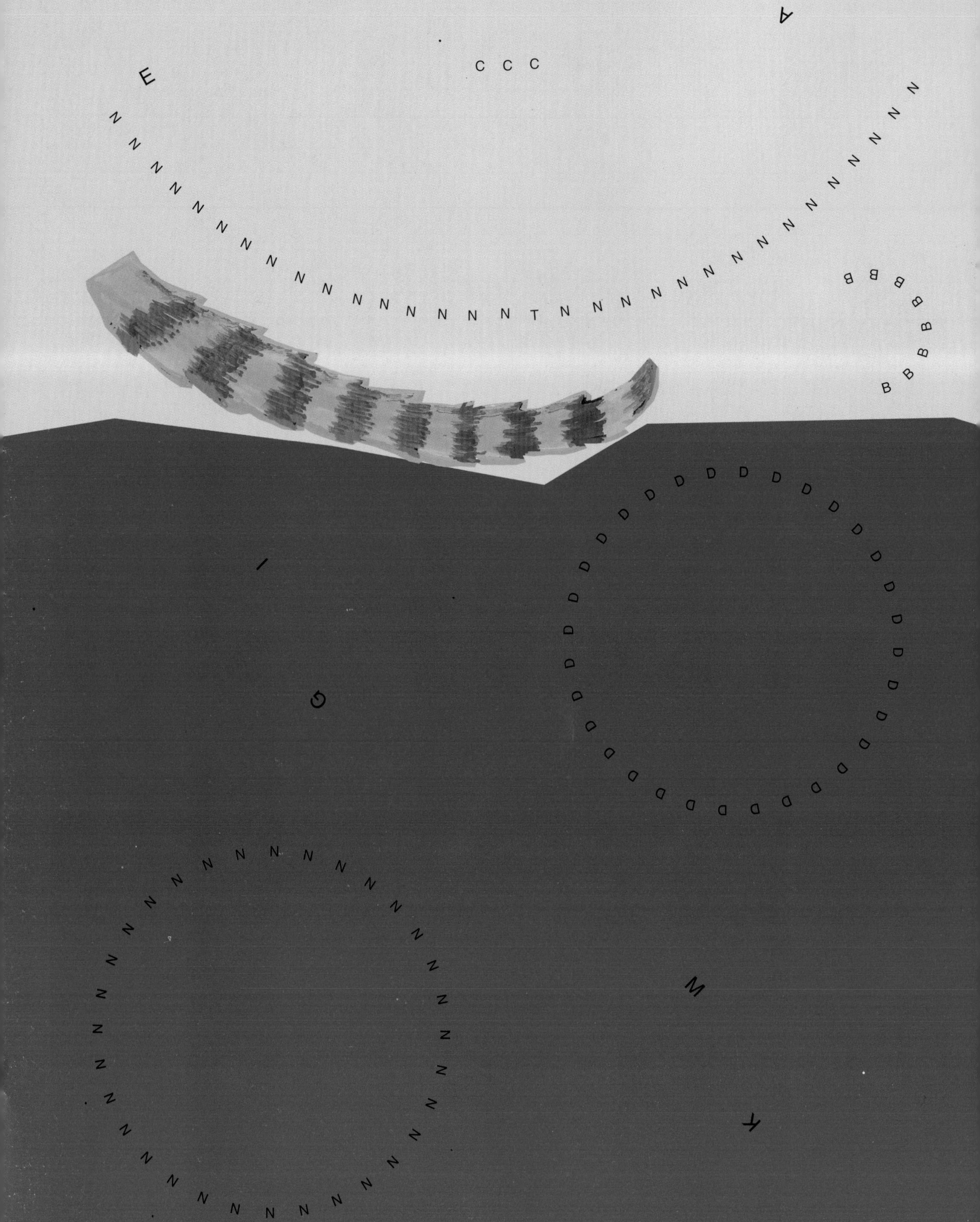
A
C C C
E
N N N N N N N N N N N N N N N N T N N N N N N N N N N N N N N N
B B B B B B B B
D D D D D D D D D D D D D D D D D D D D D D D D D D D D D D D D
I
G
M
K
N N N N N N N N N N N N N N N N N N N N N N N N N N N N N N N N

CTS

H

H

CTS

I

I

CTS

J

CTS

K

J

L

H

H

I

I

M

K

A

CTS

L

CTS

M

▼
D

▼
C

B ▶   ◀ B

▲
D

▲
C

E
▼

▲
E

A

G
▼

F
▼

▲
G

▲
F

The Frog

C C C

G

F

A

I

H

T T T T T T T T T T T T T T T T T T T T T T T T T T T T T T T T T

K

J

E E E E E E E E E E E E E E E E E E E E E E E E E E E E E

B B B B B B B B

▲

O

M

S

Q

T T T T T T T T T T T T T T T T T T T T T T T

The Mouse

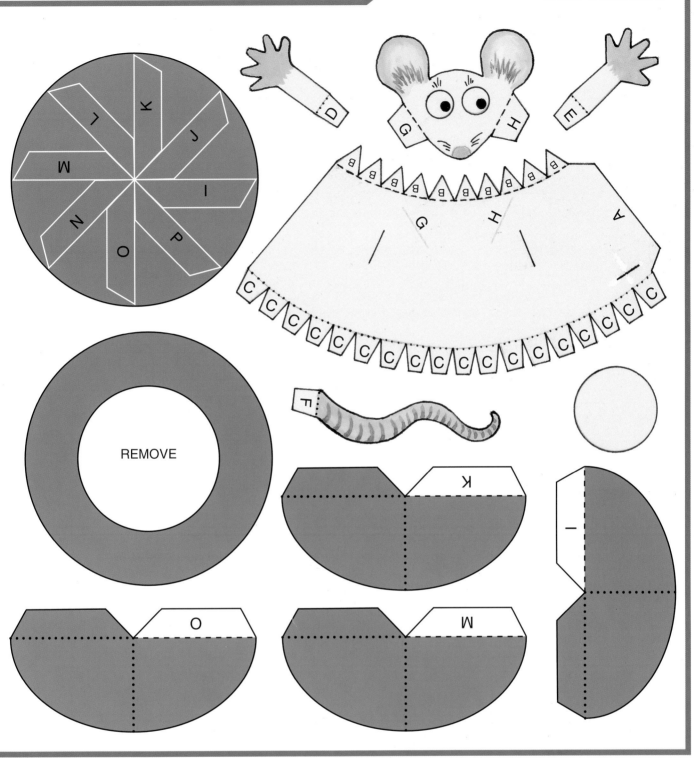

Feet for the Chickens

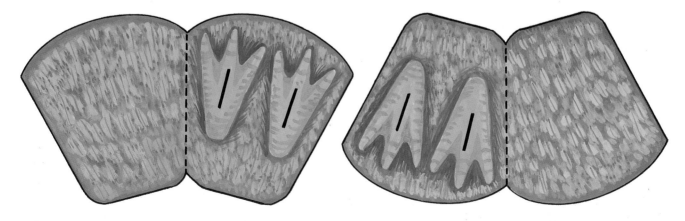

The Chickens

The Chickens' feet are on page 7.

10

The Crocodile

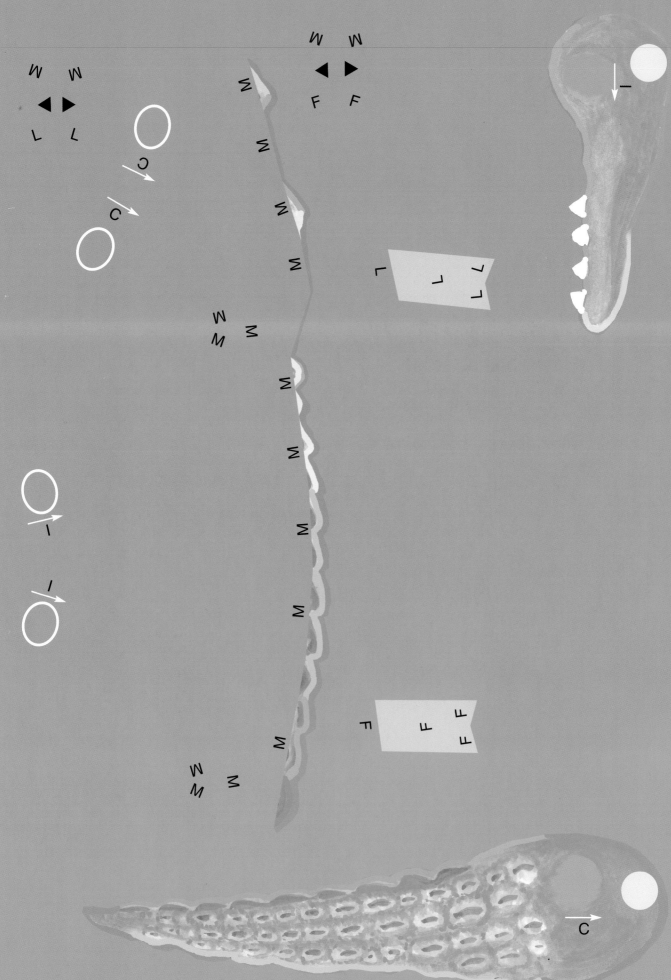

The Tiger

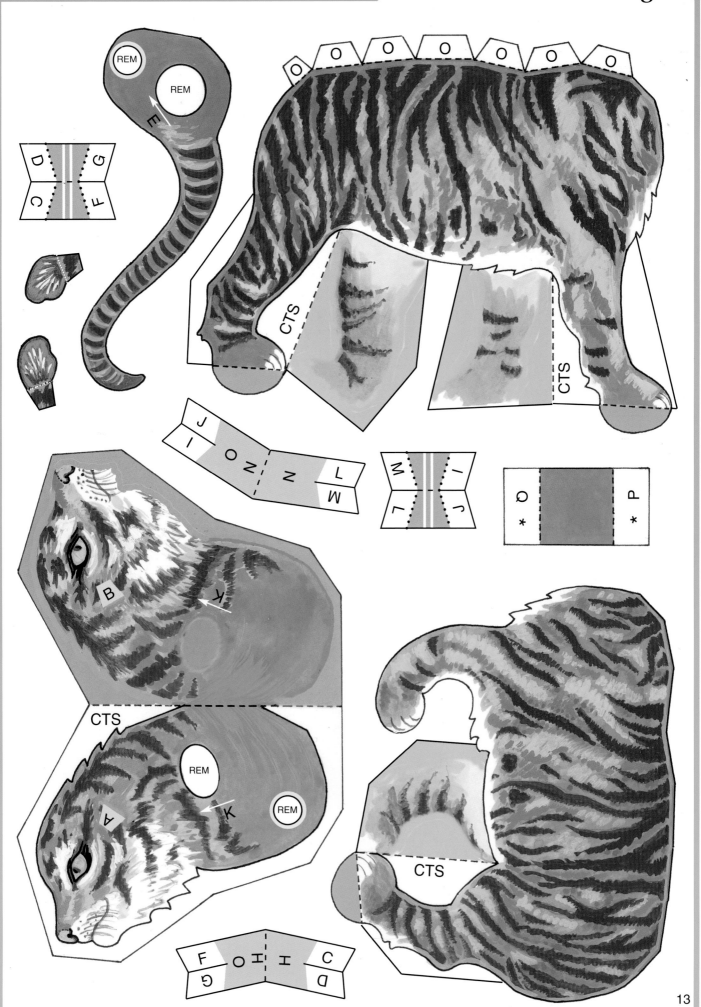

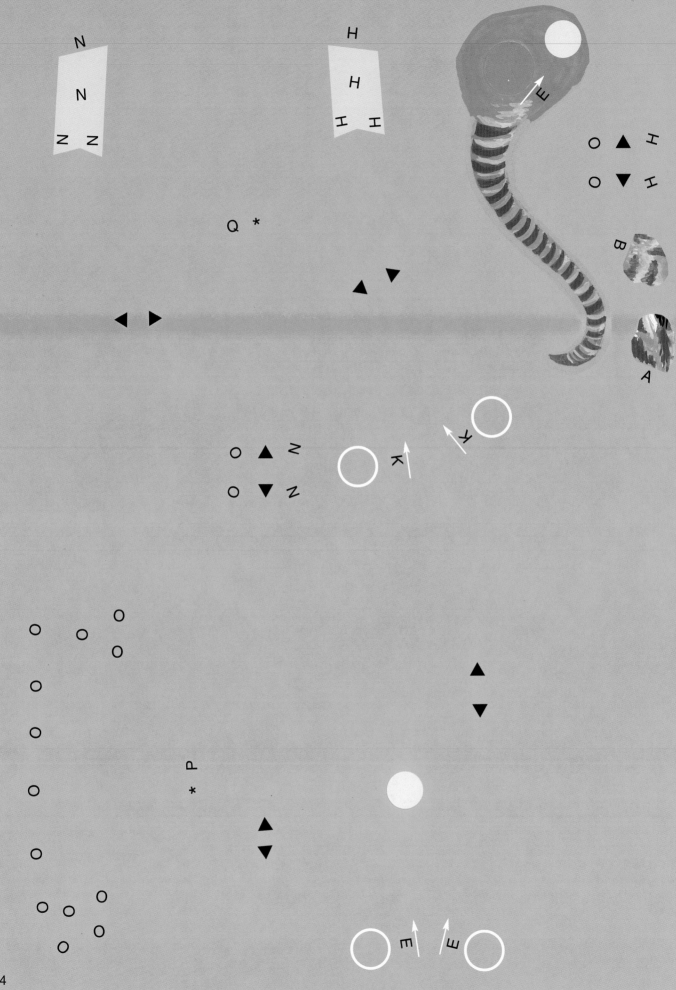

Type of Glue

To get the best results you need a glue which sets quickly but not instantly and which does not leave dirty marks. We particularly recommend a petroleum based glue such as 'UHU All Purpose', especially the 'GEL' version. 'Bostik Clear' also gives good results.

How to make good models

1. First read about the type of glue and scoring.

2. Cut out all the pieces of the model of your choice, keeping well away from the outline.

3. Score along all the score lines. They are marked as dotted lines of two kinds – – – – – – – – – – – – – – – – – and ·························

4. Cut out precisely along the cut lines which are marked as solid lines: ——————————
   Where there are holes, they are indicated by cut lines and the word 'Remove' or 'Rem'.

5. Cut around the outer cut lines of the matching frames.

Scoring

Scoring is very important if you are to make accurate models. It makes the paper fold cleanly and accurately along the line you want. Use a ball point pen which has run out of ink and press firmly along the dotted fold lines. Experienced model makers may use a craft knife, but it needs care not to cut right through the paper. When the score lines are straight, it is a good idea to use a straight edge and to score along it.

6. Fold away from you to make hill folds and towards you to make valley folds. Crease firmly along these lines.

Hill Fold   Valley Fold

7. Glue the matching frames together back to back and then cut around the outline looking at the side marked CTS meaning 'Cut This Side'.

8. Glue the sections of the model together in alphabetical order A, B, C, ... remembering to add the Blu-Tack at the proper stage. Details on the use of Blu-Tack are given on page 18.

The models fall naturally into six families or types according to the way that they move.
Now follow the special instructions for the groups.

The 'Point to Point' Movement

There is only one model which has this movement and it is made simply by following the general instructions.

Matching frames are used to make the parrots be of double thickness. Score along the score line, fold, spread glue inside one side of folded paper then press the two sides together. When paper is dry cut out the parrots while looking at the side marked CTS or 'Cut This Side'.

The Parrot Tree

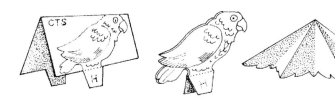

The 'umbrella' part of the tree is folded with alternate hill and valley folds.

The 'Round and Round' Movement

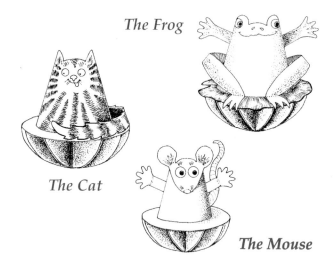

The Frog

The Cat

The Mouse

These three moving models rock on their spherical bases and if knocked return to upright or beyond.

Follow the general instructions to make them. Then squeeze a blob of glue into the point where all the four folded semicircles meet, giving extra strength just where it is needed.

Using the same base shapes why not make up some animal models of your own. Keep the figures cone shaped and add different expressions, hands, ears and tails.

The 'Heads and Tails' Movement

All four of these models move in a similar way and they are made by following the standard instructions. In addition, each of the moving parts needs some Blu-Tack for balance. Before starting to assemble each model, add the advised amount of Blu-Tack as described on page 18. When completed it may be necessary to make fine adjustments to get the moving pieces to balance and move in a more attractive way. This is best done by adding or removing small amounts of Blu-Tack.

The Cockerel   *The Hen*

The Tiger

The Crocodile

To give extra strength to the legs of the Chickens they are of double thickness. Look for the ▲ symbols.

The Tiger's legs are doubled in thickness by using matching frames, in a similar way to the parrots. Glue them back to back and when the glue is dry, cut out the legs while looking at the side marked CTS meaning 'Cut This Side'.

The 'Rock and Roll' Movement

Each of these models is made by following the standard instructions. It is important to remember to add the strip of Blu-Tack to the curved base before the sides are glued into position.

The Seal's head is intended just to push over the neck and not to be glued into place. It can then be taken off if ever you need to get at the Blu-Tack again. If you would like to change this model why not slip his head on the other way round so that it is facing his tail and lying on his back.

The Bear has a trapdoor beneath its chin so that if you want to alter the amount of Blu-Tack or change its position it is easy to get at. Push the flaps through the slits to keep it in place.

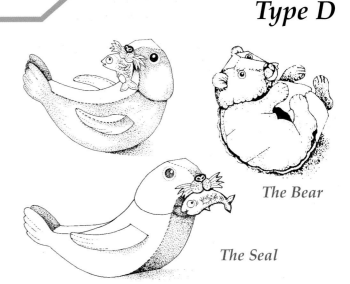

The Bear

The Seal

The 'Side to Side' Movement

The Monkey

The Crab and its Stand

Follow the standard instructions to make these two models, remembering to add the two layers of Blu-Tack to the curved base of the Monkey before the sides are glued into position.

The Monkey's head is not attached to the body but rests on a horizontal neck-like support. The head moves from side to side in a most attractive way as the model rocks on its base. Two layers of Blu-Tack in the base means that the Monkey moves back and forth very easily. If you need to adjust the Blu-Tack later, it can be reached through the trapdoor.

The Crab has no need of Blu-Tack but balances and rocks on its stand with a side to side movement suggesting the scuttling motion of a real crab.

When the legs are cut out you may find it easier using only your fingers to pinch the hill and valley folds rather than score them. The legs can be left fairly flat with shallow folds or make sharp folds so the legs are hunched up.

The 'To and Fro' Movement

These final models are the ones which are the most difficult to make but are certainly also the most satisfying. It is wise to leave them until last as they make use of several of the techniques of earlier models.

The Owl

The Penguins

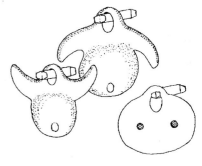

The Penguins' arms and the Owl's eyes are on special hangers. This construction is similar to the heads and tails of Type

Follow the standard instructions and always work in alphabetical order. It is most important that the hanger is threaded over its support at the correct stage and it has been given a letter to indicate when this should be. The directions of the white arrows show which way round they go. Each of the models has a two-layer strip of Blu-Tack at its base to provide stability.

Extra Weight

The models of the moving menagerie are made entirely from paper and to make some of them balance and move in an interesting way extra weight is needed in just the right places. We suggest the use of Blu-Tack for this purpose. However it would be possible to use plasticine.

Blu-Tack cuts very easily and conveniently with scissors and that is the easiest way to get the right quantity.

The Blu-Tack Quantity Guides below indicate how much is needed for the models They are for Blu-Tack of a standard thickness.

4mm

If you have a new packet, you will probably find that it is already that thickness. If not, or if you are going to recycle some older Blu-Tack, smooth or roll it to be 4mm thick.

Using Blu-Tack for Balance

Certain moving pieces hang from horizontal supports and need extra weight so that they balance correctly. Blu-Tack is the best material to use.

 A pale blue circle around a hole marked 'rem' indicates that the Blu-Tack has to be pushed through the hole and then flattened on both sides. This means that the weight is both distributed centrally and is also very unlikely ever to fall out.

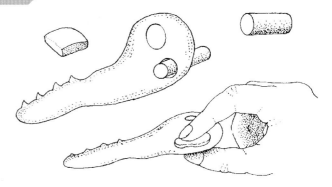

Blu-Tack Quantity Guides

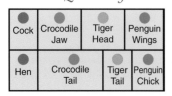

Cock	Crocodile Jaw	Tiger Head	Penguin Wings
Hen	Crocodile Tail	Tiger Tail	Penguin Chick

Assuming the standard thickness of 4mm.

1. Cut the advised amount of Blu-Tack and roll it into a fat cylinder.
2. Push it through the hole in the hanger.
3. Squeeze it gently between your finger and thumb to make a 'rivet' shape.

Using Blu-Tack for Rocking Movement

For some models, Blu-Tack provides the weight necessary at the lowest point to ensure that the model rocks back and forth in a stable way about its upright position.

Cut the advised amount of Blu-tack of standard thickness and press it on to the marked area, before the body of the animal is completed. The amount of Blu-Tack should be about right and there is always a flap or trapdoor which gives access to it for later adjustments.

Some models rock better if there is a second layer of Blu-Tack at the centre of the base, just inside the trapdoor. Experiment until you get a good rolling effect.

Although Blu-Tack does not dry out easily, it may do so after a long period and the trapdoors then allow access to it.

Blu-Tack Quantity Guides

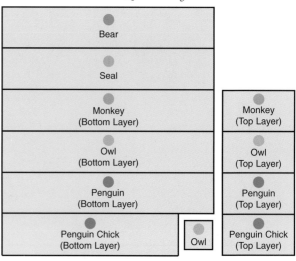

Bear	
Seal	
Monkey (Bottom Layer)	Monkey (Top Layer)
Owl (Bottom Layer)	Owl (Top Layer)
Penguin (Bottom Layer)	Penguin (Top Layer)
Penguin Chick (Bottom Layer) / Owl	Penguin Chick (Top Layer)

Assuming the standard thickness of 4mm.

Optional Blu-Tack Covers

Blu-Tack generally does not stick to skin and so it is usually a simple matter to press it into its allotted place. However, it is a strange fact that on some occasions and for some people the Blu-Tack does stick to fingers and so it is difficult to let go. If that is the case, cut out and use the optional Blu-Tack covers on page 31 before pressing the Blu-Tack into place. They can be left in situ in case adjustment is needed later on.

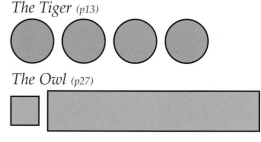

The Tiger (p13)

The Owl (p27)

The full set of covers is on page 31.

The Bear

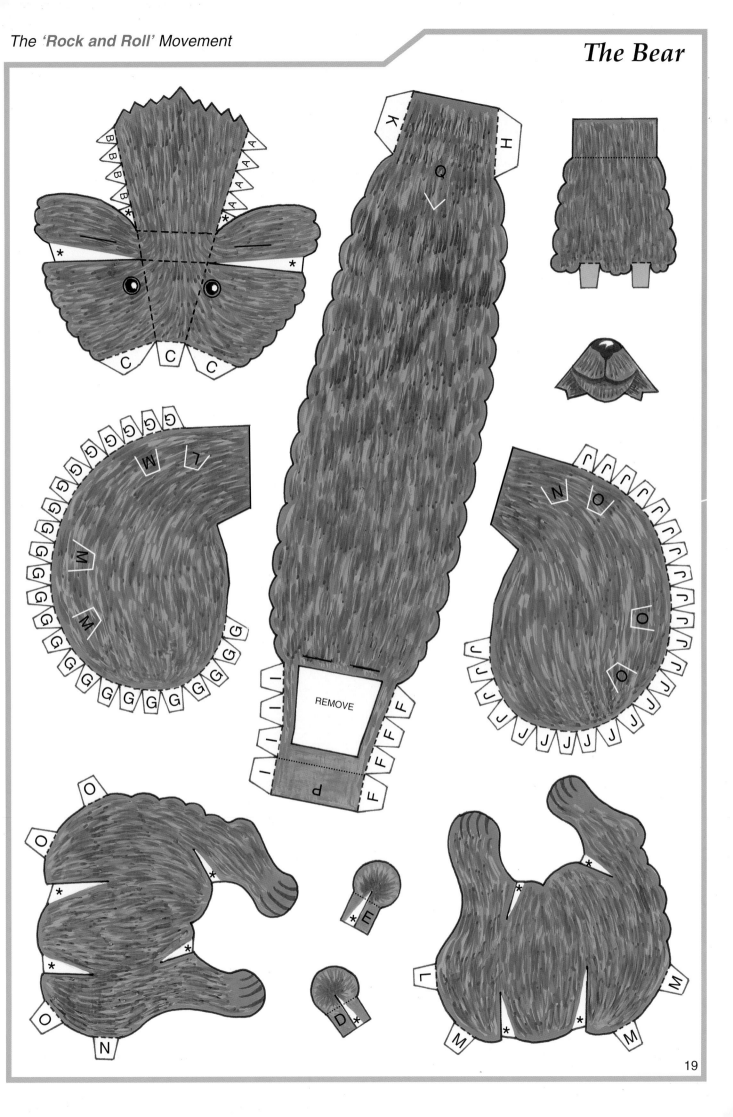

REMOVE

Weight here

The Seal

Match the arrows

Match the arrows

Match the arrows

Match
the arrows

Weight
here

The Crab

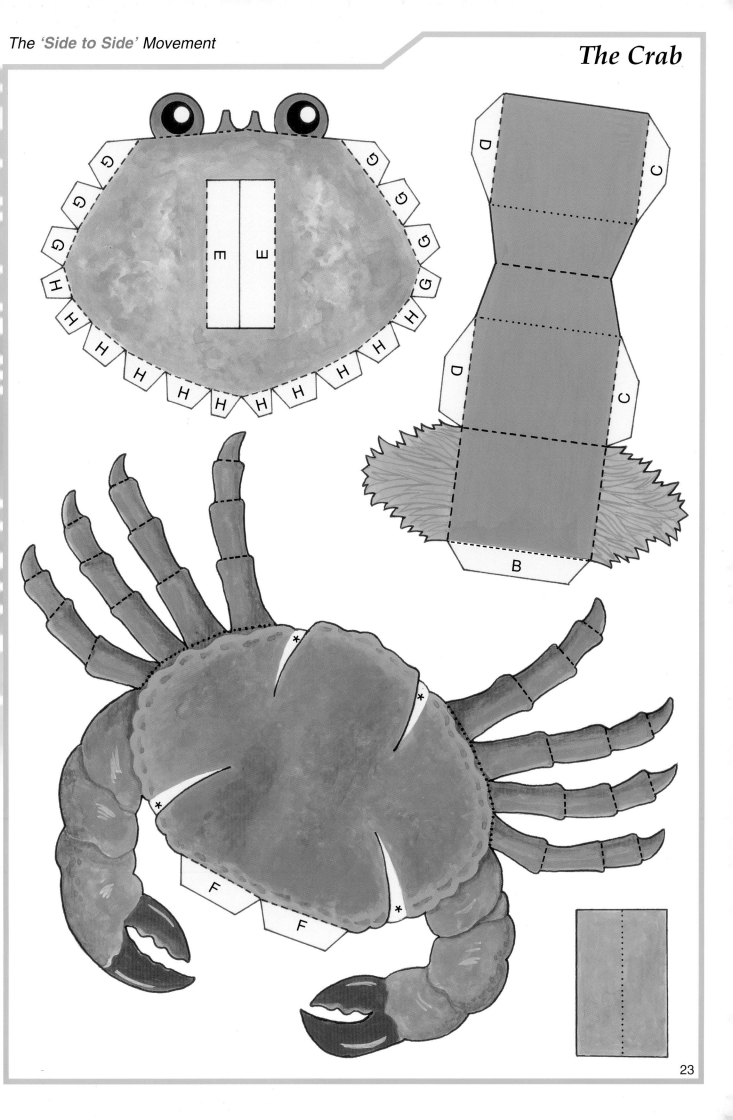

B

F   F

A
▼
▲
A

D

C   D

C

H* H H H*
H   H
H   H H
H   G
H   G G
H
H   G *
G   G
G * G

E   E

24

The Monkey

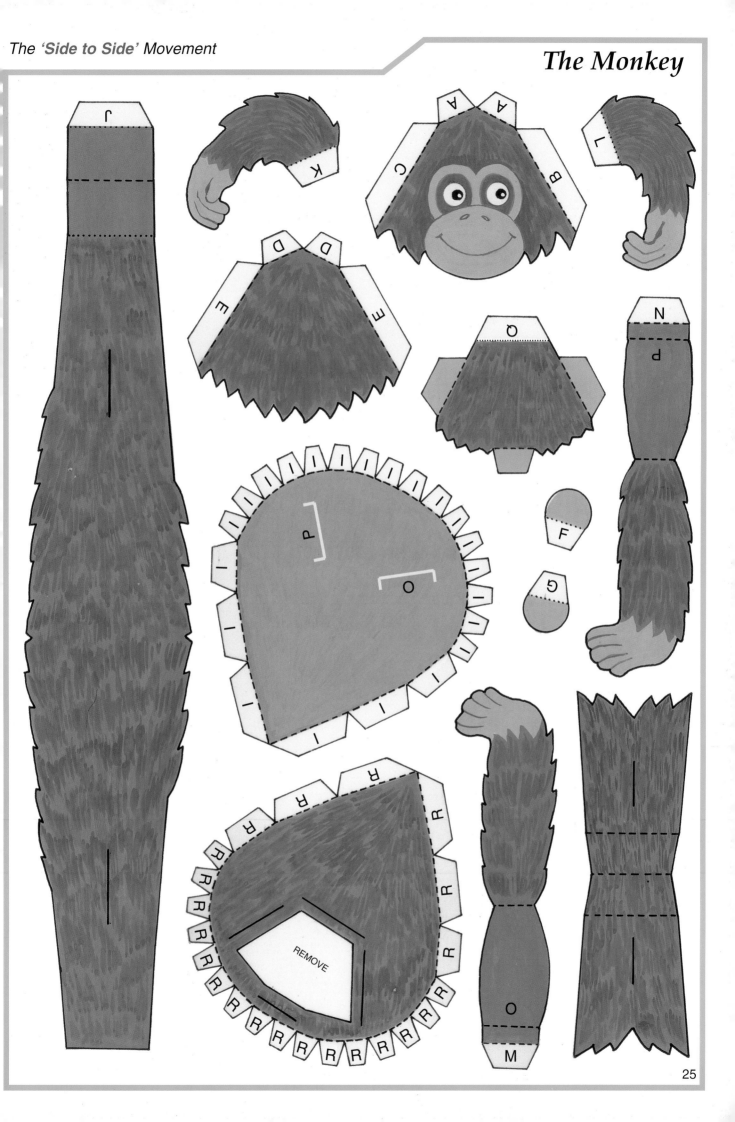

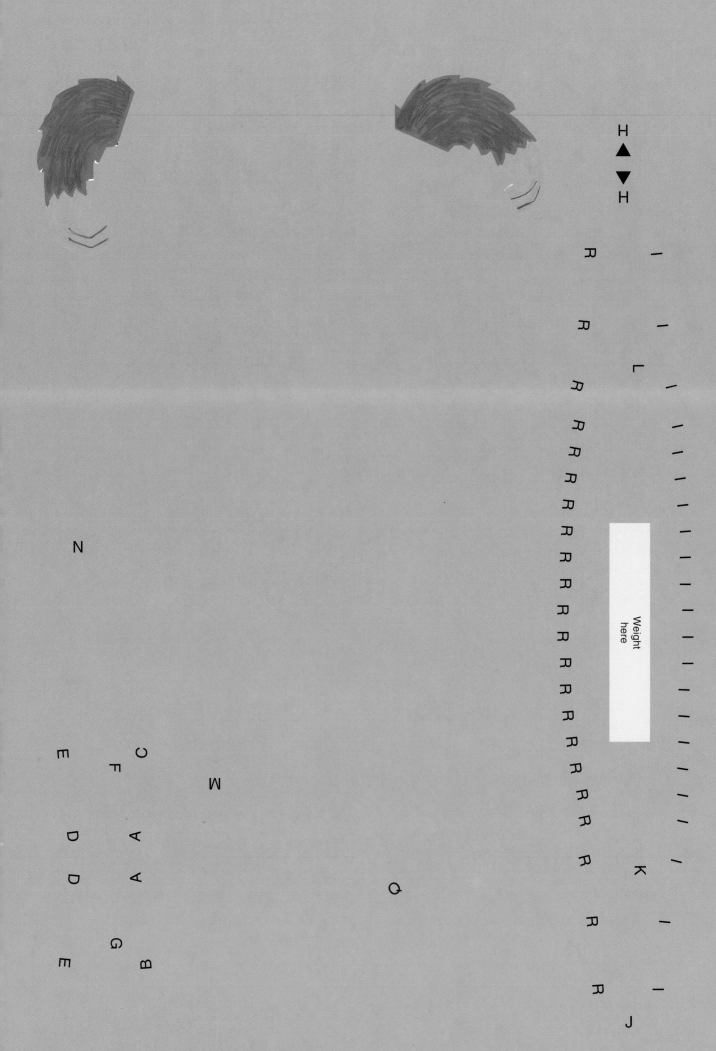

Weight here

H ▲ ▼ H

26

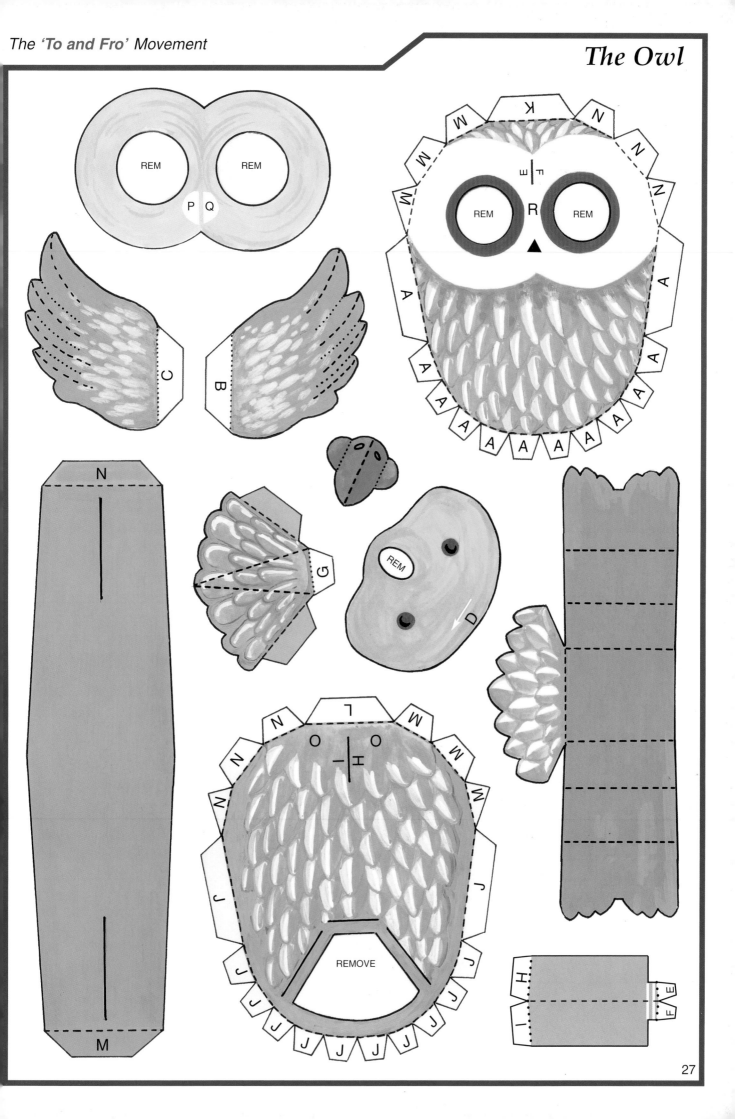

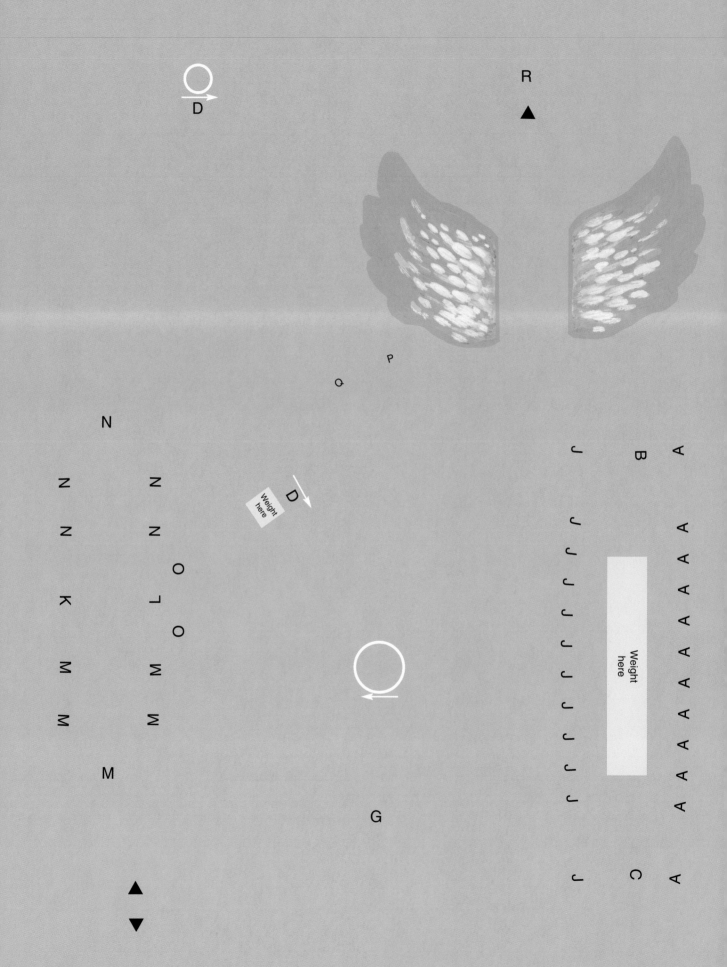

The Penguin

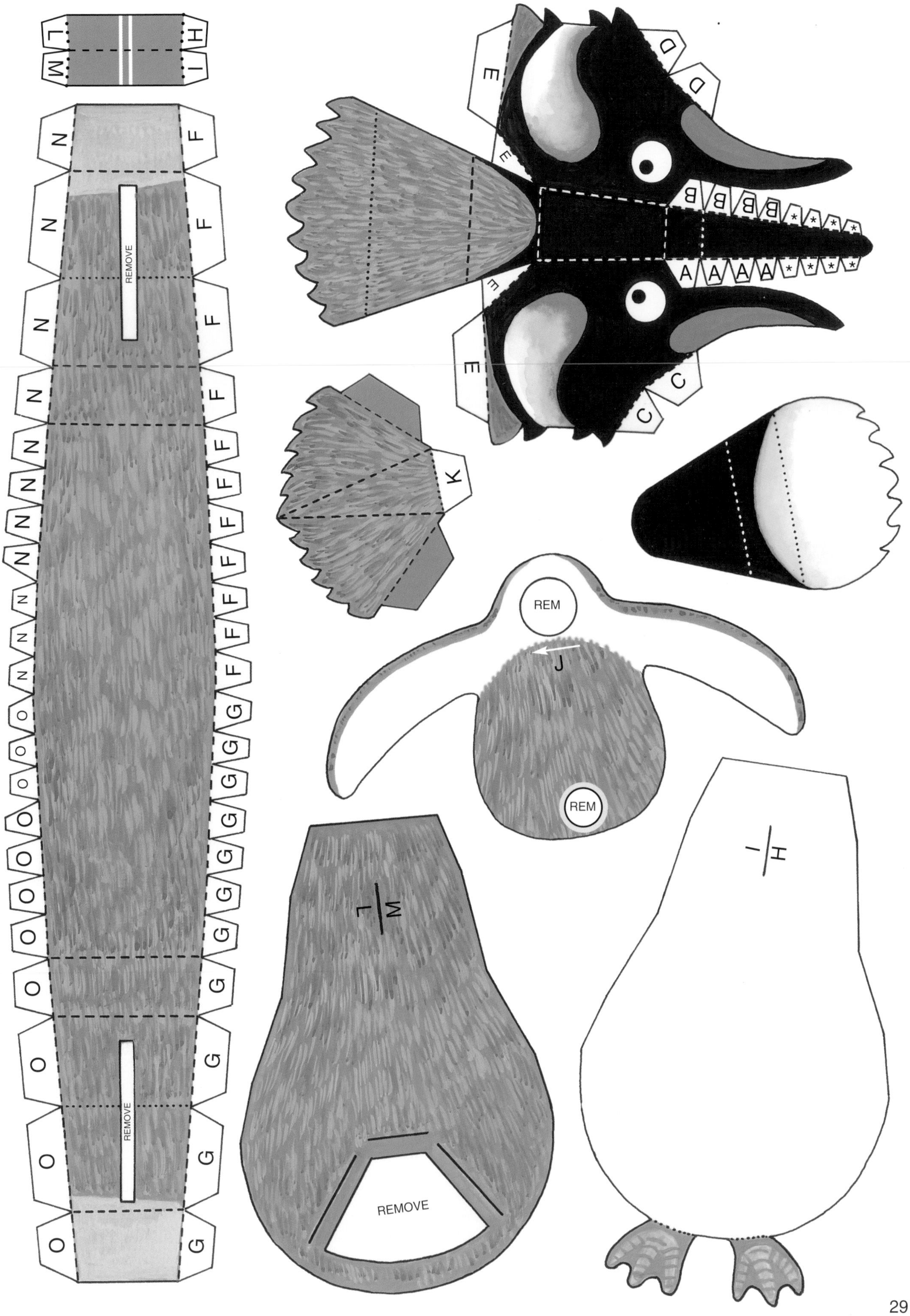

L | H

M | H

N | F

N | F REMOVE

N | F

N | F

N | F

N | F

N | F

N | F

O | F

O | G

O | G

O | G

O | G

O | G

O | G REMOVE

O | G

E | D

E | D

E | B B B *

A A A A * * *

E | C

E | C

K

REM

J

REM

L / M

H

REMOVE

* * * * B B B B B

E
E
E
E

* * * * A A A A A

D
D D

C C

J →

Weight
here

G

○

F

J →

○

O

N

G

F

J ←

N

G

F

O

N

G

O

K

N

G

F

O

N

G

F

F

O

N

G

F

O

N

G G G G G F F F F F O O O O O O N N N N

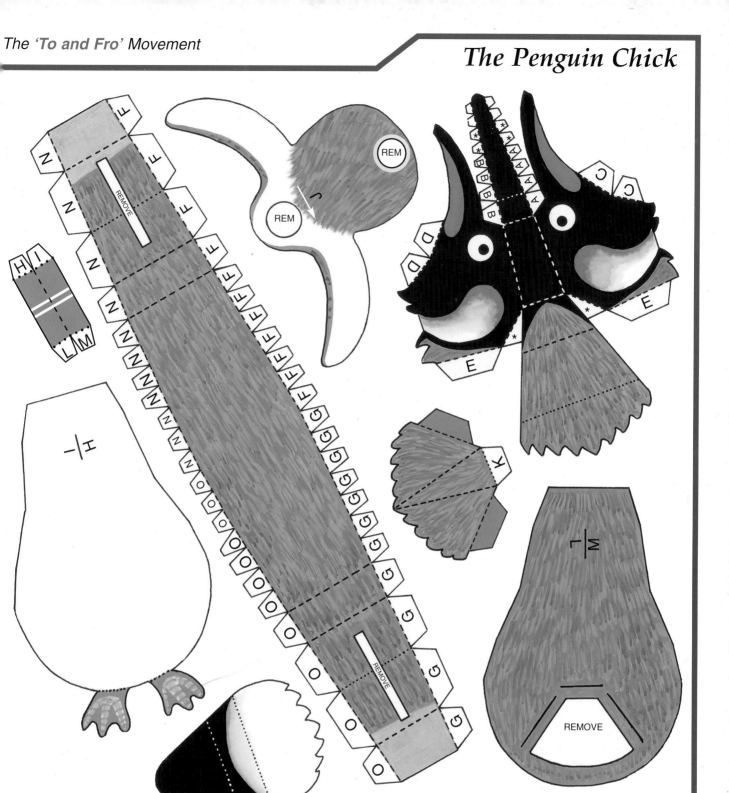

Weight Covers (optional)

The Chickens (p9)

The Bear (p19)

The Owl (p27)

The Crocodile (p11)

The Monkey (p19)

The Penguins (p29 & 31)

The Tiger (p13)

The Seal (p19)

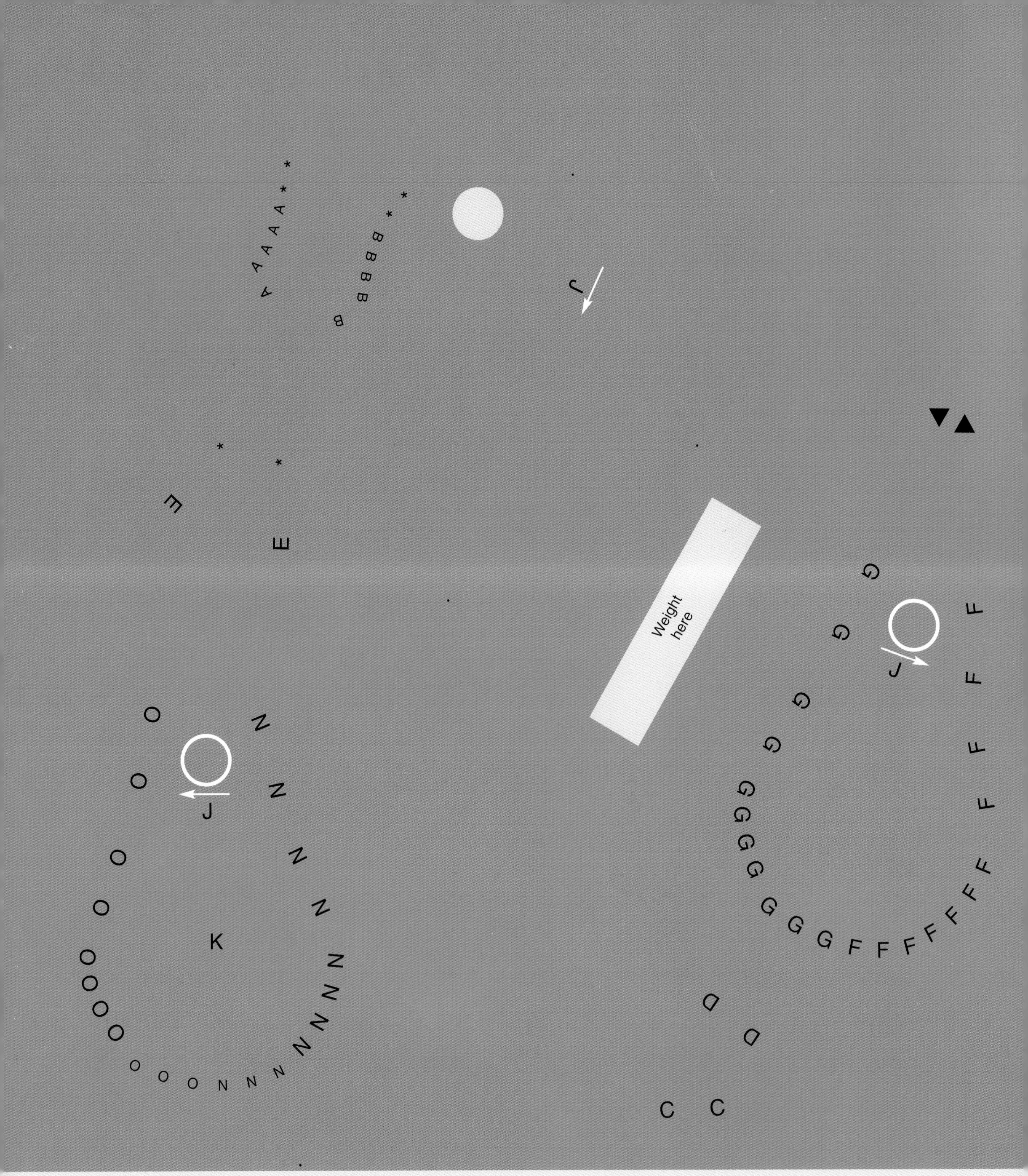

Weight here

A A A A * *
*
B
B
B
B
*
*

J

E
E
*
*

▼▲

O
O
N
O
J
N
N
K
N
O
N
O
N
O
N
O
o N
O o o N N N

G
G
G
G
J
G
F
G
F
G
F
G
F
G
F
G G F F F F
G G F
D
D
D
C C

32